Troll Tales
Teacher Resources
Oscar and Otto

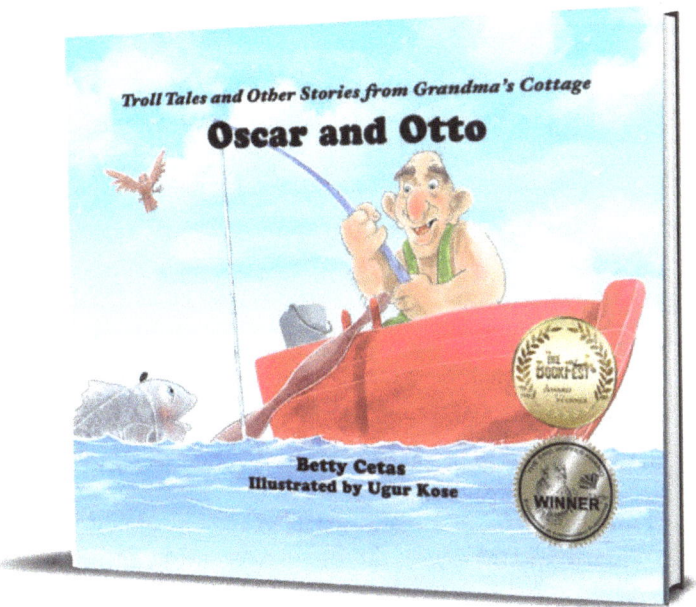

Betty Cetas
Amanda M. Cetas

Windy Sea Publishing

Windy Sea Publishing, LLC
Tucson, Arizona
www.windyseapublishing.com

Table of Contents

TROLL TALES CURRICULUM (Ages 4-8)

Overview

- **Subject Areas**: Language Arts, Art, Social Studies, Science, Character Education
- **Format**: Unit study (5 day plan)
- **Themes**: Finnish culture, character development, nature exploration, creative storytelling
- **Tone**: Family-friendly, secular, imaginative

Unit Study: *Oscar and Otto*

Target Age: 4-8 (Preschool to 2nd Grade)

Subjects: Language Arts, Art, Character Ed, Social Studies, Science

Focus Themes:

- Friendship
- Loyalty
- Communication
- Learning from mistakes

Weekly Lesson Planner

Day 1: Read the book aloud. Discuss Oscar and Otto's relationship.

Day 2: Teach new vocabulary words with flash cards and a word-definition matching game.

Day 3: Character education lesson about empathy, respect, kindness, responsibility.

Day 4: Science Experiment: Why Does Ice Float?

Day 5: Social Studies: What is Ice Fishing and When Did it Start?

Printables Included

1. Vocabulary matching worksheet
2. Science experiment observation sheet
3. Ice fishing timeline

4. Finland and Europe outline maps
5. Emotion and behavioral identification cards

Language Arts Activities

- Comprehension discussion questions
- Vocabulary matching worksheet
- Dialogue practice: writing what Oscar and Otto might say to each other
- Creative writing prompt: "My favorite thing to do is …"
- Retelling the story with puppets or drawings

Science & Social Studies

- Science Lesson: "Why Does Ice Float?"
- Social Studies & Cultural Lesson: "What is Ice Fishing?" and "Why Do People Ice Fish?"
- Learning to read and use maps

Art & Expression

- Create a troll mask (paper plate, yarn/string, crayons).
- Draw the forest setting and Oscar's expression.
- Build a mini forest diorama using natural or craft materials.

Character Development

- Discuss forgiveness and being a good friend.
- Emotion tree activity: how do the characters feel before/after?
- Kindness role-play: saying sorry, helping others

Final Project Ideas

- Write a new Oscar and Otto adventure.
- Friendship storybook or puppet show
- Poster of "How to Be a Good Friend"

Day 1 Lesson

1. **Read the book, *Oscar and Otto*, aloud.**

2. **Discussion Questions:**
   - What did Oscar want to do at the beginning of the story?
   - What did Otto want to do in the beginning?

- How did their different wants (or goals) lead to trouble (or conflict) between them?

- What happened to cause each of them to see the other differently?

- Why was friendship better than fighting in this story?

- Can you think of a time in your life when you were angry with someone? Why were you angry? What happened? Did you make up?

- Do you agree that friendship is better than fighting? Why or why not?

- Do you think it better to stand up to bullies, run away, or stand firm and take what comes? Are there any other options?

  NOTE: Give a longer "wait time" with questions 7 and 8. Encourage students/children to really think about it and weigh the consequences. If a student thinks it is better to fight or hold a grudge, help them to see the trouble that may come from these behaviors.

  There is a difference between fighting with family and friends and being picked on by bullies. This is a good opportunity to talk about these differences and how children should handle these situations.

2. Creative Writing prompt:

"My favorite thing to do is ..."

Day 2 Lesson

1. Vocabulary Word Lesson
- Using 3" x 5" index card or a folded sheet of lined paper with the vocabulary words listed on half of the paper, have students look up the definition for each vocabulary word and write it on the backside of each card or on the other half of the paper across from the appropriate word.

  Vocabulary Words:

Nibbled	Delicious	Clever	Teased	Pranks
Confused	Plotted	Miserable	Emerged	Bragging

  Then have students (or the teacher) quiz them by reading or holding up a word and having the student give the definition.

- To reinforce the vocabulary words either on the same day, or at a later time, print out the word matching worksheet.

  Have your child/student complete the vocabulary matching worksheet (pages 15-16) by drawing a line from the vocabulary word to the appropriate definition.

Day 3 Lesson

Topic: *Teasing, Bragging, and Pranking*

Duration: 30-45 minutes
Core Values: Empathy, Respect, Kindness, Responsibility

LEARNING OBJECTIVES

By the end of the lesson, students will be able to:

- Recognize what teasing, bragging, and pranking look and sound like.
- Understand how these behaviors make others feel.
- Learn kind and respectful alternatives to hurtful behavior.

Practice empathy through storytelling, role-play, and reflection.

Lesson Outline

1. Warm-Up Discussion (5–7 minutes)

Prompt: "Has someone ever made you feel left out, laughed at you, or told you they were better than you?"

Let children share brief stories or feelings. Validate emotions and gently introduce the terms:

- **Teasing** = Saying something to make fun of someone
- **Bragging** = Saying things just to show off or feel better than others
- **Pranking** = Doing something "funny" that might hurt or upset someone else
- **Helping** = Doing something "nice" to benefit someone else

Visual Aid: Use the images of Otto provided with the "Behavior Cards" (found on pages 25-29) to show examples of each.

2. Story Time (10 minutes)

Reread *Oscar and Otto* and point out the times when Otto:

- Teases Oscar
- Brags to the other fish
- Plays a prank on Oscar

Ask:

- How did Oscar or the other fish feel?
- Was that kind or unkind?
- What could Otto have done instead?

3. Interactive Activity: Feelings Sorting Game (5–10 minutes)

Prepare the "Emotion Identification Cards" and have students identify the emotion each character is feeling. Optional: Ask them to explain what clues tell them that the character is feeling (fill in the specific emotion)?

Note: This activity is especially good for younger children, or children who struggle with reading social/emotional clues in others.

4. Role-Play: What Should We Do? (10 minutes)

Using the "Behavioral Cards" have children/students sort each into:

- **Kind**
- **Not Kind**

Ask students to explain what is happening in the image and why they put it in the kind or unkind pile.

Then discuss how each unkind situation could be changed to show kindness.

Alternatively: Have students make character puppets using paper lunch sacks and markers. Give pairs of students simple scripts to act out teasing, bragging, pranking scenes using their puppets.

Then ask:

- "How were they being unkind?
- "How could we fix it?"
- "What words can we use to be kind?"

Then, have them reenact a scene where Oscar and Otto solve their problem.

5. Creative Expression (Optional Extension)

- **Draw a Kind Troll or Fish** who helps friends feel included.
- **Make a "Kindness Toolbox"**: Fill with phrases like "Do you want to play?" or "That's cool you did that!"

CLOSING REFLECTION

Ask:

- "What will you do if someone teases you?"
- "What can you say if you feel like bragging?"

Create a class **Kindness Pledge** or mural with drawings or handprints.

Day 4 Lesson

Conduct a science experiment to answer the question: "Why Does Ice Float?"

Big Question: Why does ice float in water instead of sinking like most solids?

Duration: 30-40 minutes

KEY SCIENCE CONCEPT:

- Ice is **less dense** than liquid water, so it **floats**!
- When water freezes, it **expands**, taking up more space and becoming lighter for its size.

Lesson Outline

1. Engage (Discussion & Prediction) (5 minutes)

Ask:

- "What happens when you put a rock in water? What about a plastic toy?"
- "What do you think will happen if we put ice in water?"

Let children make predictions!

2. Explore (Hands-On Experiment) (10–15 minutes)

Materials:

- Clear container (glass, jar, bucket)
- Water
- Ice cubes
- Small rocks or coins (for comparison)
- Food coloring (optional, for fun visuals)

Steps:

1. Fill the glass with water.
2. Gently place an ice cube into the water. Watch what happens!
3. Drop in a small rock or coin and compare: Which one sinks? Which floats?
4. Have students record their observations on the "Science Experiment Observation Sheet."
5. (Optional) Add a drop of food coloring to see how water moves around the ice.

Ask:

- "Where is the ice cube?"

- "Is it floating all the way or just part of it?"
- "Why do you think that is?"

3. Explanation (Simple Physics) (5 minutes)

Tell them:

- "Ice is made of water, but when water freezes, it spreads out and takes up more space. That means it gets lighter for its size, or *less dense*. That's why ice floats!"
- Use hands to show "tight" molecules in water vs. "spread out" molecules in ice (great visual!)
  - Optional: *Magic School Bus* Season 2, Episode 5: "Wet All Over" is a great resource to explain why this occurs!
- "Ice is different (anomalous) compared to other solids in becoming less dense. Most, if not all, other solids become *denser* when going from their liquid to solid forms."

Ask:

- "Why do you think this difference is good?" (In fact, it is absolutely critical for life on Earth!)
- **Answer:** "If ice became denser, it would sink to the bottom of the lakes and oceans, causing all the water to get colder and freeze. There would be no water left for fish or animals to live in. Earth would become a giant ice ball. Even the summer sun would not be enough to melt the oceans and lakes. As a result, there would be no life on Earth!"

4. Extend (Creative Learning Options) (5–10 minutes)

- **Draw** what they saw: a picture of a floating ice cube and a sinking rock.
- **Write or dictate** a short answer: "Ice floats because..."
- **Melt it**: Watch the ice melt and see how it turns back to water.

Learning Outcome:

Children will understand that **ice floats because it is less dense than water**, and they will have observed it in a safe, hands-on way.

Day 5 Lesson

Big Questions:

- What is **ice fishing**?
- Why do people fish through the ice in cold places like Finland?
- How and why has it been done **through history**?

Duration: 30-45 minutes

1. Introduction: *What Is Ice Fishing?* (5 minutes)

Tell children:

"In very cold places, lakes freeze in the winter. But under the ice, water stays liquid — and fish still swim around! Ice fishing means cutting a hole in the ice and fishing from above!"

Show a photo or illustration of *(images are on pages 18-19)*:

- A frozen lake
- A hole in the ice
- A person ice fishing

Ask:

- "Have you ever seen ice on a lake?"
- "What do you think people need to stay warm on the ice?"

2. History & Culture: *Why Do People Ice Fish: From Survival to Sport?* (7-10 minutes)

Tell them:

"People in northern places like **Finland, Canada, and Alaska** have ice fished for a very long time, ever since humans first arrived in these places. Finland is known for its abundant lakes and seas. Long ago, humans learned to cut holes in the frozen lakes to **get food in the winter**. Today, people still ice fish for food — and for fun!"

Early Origins & Survival (Over 2000 years ago):

- Ice fishing emerged as a way for indigenous groups (local or native people) to access food during the winter when open water fishing was impossible.
- People used hand tools (like chisels) to cut through the ice.
- Then they used spears to catch fish that swam close to the holes.
- Wooden or bone decoys were used to attract the fish.
- They wore fur clothes to stay warm.

100 Years Ago:

- People used hand drills and simple fishing rods.
- Ice fishing was still a way to get food, but some people were also ice fishing for fun!
- Families started going out together to enjoy the wilderness and nature.
- Ice fishing started to become a popular sport.

Today:

- Ice fishing is still done in **Finland and other northern places.**

- People might use ice augers (drills) to make holes
- They use fishing rods and bring **tiny huts with heaters** onto the ice!
- Some even use underwater cameras.
- Ice fishing is now both a **tradition and a hobby**.

3. Think & Talk (5-10 minutes)

- "How do you think people came up with the idea of ice fishing?"
- "What is the same about ice fishing from when it began, to 100 years ago, and today?" (*continuity over time*)
- "What has changed about ice fishing from when it began, to 100 years ago, and today?" (*change over time*)
- "Would you want to try it?"

4. Creative Activity (Choose One) (10-15 minutes)

A. *Draw the Timeline* (Worksheet is on page 20.)

- Provide three boxes labeled: Long Ago, 100 Years Ago, Today
- Let children draw what ice fishing looked like in each time

B. *Pretend Play: Ice Fishing Station*

- Use a blue sheet and cut "ice holes" from paper
- Let kids "fish" using strings, magnets, or laminated paper fish

C. *Mini Craft: Ice Fishing Hut*

- Make small huts from tissue boxes or paper
- Add cotton for snow and cut-out people ice fishing

Optional Extension: *Cultural Connection to Finland*

Explain:

"In Finland, ice fishing is called *pilkkiminen* (pronounced **píl**-ki-mi-něn). This word is completely different from the Finnish word for fishing – *kalastus* (pronounced **ka**-la-stoos)."

Ask:

- "Why do you think these words are so different in Finnish?"
- "What do you think that tells us about their culture?"

"Many families still go ice fishing in the winter, especially in the northern region of Finland, which is called Lapland. Ice fishing is part of their culture and connection to nature."

Show Finland on a world map and then using the outline map provided, have students color the region known as Lapland. (It is the northern-most region.)

Lapland is also where reindeer and many other animals live.

NOTE: This ties to the Day 3 Lesson about the animals of Finland found in **Troll Tales Teacher Resources for *Oscar and the Awful, Horrible Smell*.**

For older children, have them locate Helsinki, the capital of Finland, on a world map and add it to their outline map.

Ask:

- Why do you think the capital is located there?
- What advantages does that location provide?
- Which three countries share a border with Finland?
- Which seas border Finland?

Alternatively: Using the outline map of Europe have students locate Finland and color it.

Wrap-Up (5 minutes)

Ask:

- "Why did people start ice fishing long ago?"
- "How is it different today?"
- "What tools do we have now that help us?"

ADDITIONAL UNIT IDEAS

Story Time & Discussion

- Read aloud or listen to the story multiple times throughout the week.
- Discuss main characters, setting, and the problem/solution.
- Discuss applications to personal situations.

Questions to ask:

- What was your favorite part?
- How did the characters feel? How did they change?
- What would you do if you were in this story?

Language Arts Focus

- **Vocabulary Words**: Choose 3–5 new or fun words from the story (e.g., bragging, confused, plotted, delicious).
- **Comprehension**: Simple Q&A, sequencing activities, retelling in own words.
- **Creative Writing Prompt** (adapt by age):
  - Draw and write your own troll character.
  - "What would I do if I saw someone pranking another child?"
  - Finish the sentence: "Otto bragged because…"

Cultural Connection – Finland

- Compare the location of Finland to where you live. How does Finland's latitude and longitude compare to yours? What will that mean for weather conditions (temperature, rainfall, etc.) or time zones?
- Fun facts: language, landscapes, animals (lynx, reindeer, bears), weather.
- Basic intro to Finnish folklore traditions (neutral tone).

Science or Nature Study

- Research one aquatic animal native to Finnish lakes.
- Go on a local nature walk: "What would live in our ecosystem (environment)?"
- Visit an aquarium to learn about the fish and animals that live in lakes and rivers.

Art & Expression

- Draw a lake scene from the book.
- Make a "Fish Puppet" using paper bags, markers, or colored paper.
- Create a troll storybook with drawings and simple sentences.

Character Building & Social-Emotional Learning

- Discuss themes like kindness, bravery, honesty, or problem-solving.
- Role-play scenes: "What would be a kind thing to do?"
- Draw a "Feelings Forest" where each tree represents a different emotion.

Final Project

- Diorama of a scene from the story.
- Short puppet show retelling the story.
- Poster of your fish character with labels and personality traits.

Vocabulary Matching Worksheet
Emerging Reader

Draw a line or write the matching letter that means the *opposite* of the word on the left.

1. Bragging

A. Happy (Joyful)

2. Confused

B. Yucky

3. Delicious

C. Caring

4. Clever

D. Humble

5. Miserable

E. Submerged

F. Certain (Understood)

6. Teased

7. Emerged

G. Foolish

Vocabulary Matching Worksheet
Early Reader

Draw a line or write the matching letter for each word to its correct definition.

1. Pranks

2. Bragging

3. Nibbled

4. Confused

5. Delicious

6. Plotted

7. Clever

8. Miserable

9. Teased

10. Emerged

A. Tricks or jokes played on someone thought to be funny.

B. Not sure what is happening or what something means.

C. Made fun of someone in a mean way.

D. Smart in a creative way.

E. Tastes good.

F. Talking about yourself in a way that shows off.

G. Secretly planned something.

H. Very sad or unhappy.

I. Ate something with small bites.

J. Came out from somewhere or appeared.

Science Experiment Observation Sheet

Why Does Ice Float?

In this experiment, we will see what happens when we put ice in water.

What do you think will happen to the ice?

My Prediction: _____

_____

Materials I Used:

☐ Clear container (glass, cup or jar)
☐ Water
☐ Ice cube
☐ Small rock or coin
☐ Food coloring (optional)

What Happened?

What did the ice cube do in the water? _____

What did the rock or coin do? _____

What did the food coloring show (if used)? _____

Draw what you saw:

```




```

What I Learned:

Ice floats because it is _____ than water.

Images for: *What Is Ice Fishing?*

Image of a frozen lake, by Antoloji, 17 January 2020. Licensed under the Creative Commons
Attribution-Share Alike 4.0 International

Image of ice fishing hole, by Brücke-Osteuropa, 12 February 2006. Public Domain.

Ice Fishing on the Bay of Porkkala on December 6rth, 1956, by Erkki Voutilainen (1914-1988).
Licensed under the Creative Commons

Ice Fishing Timeline

Draw what ice fishing looked like in each time period. Think about the tools they used, clothes, huts, and the lake!

Long Ago

100 Years Ago

Today

www.windyseapublishing.com

Windy Sea Publishing

Outline Map of Finland

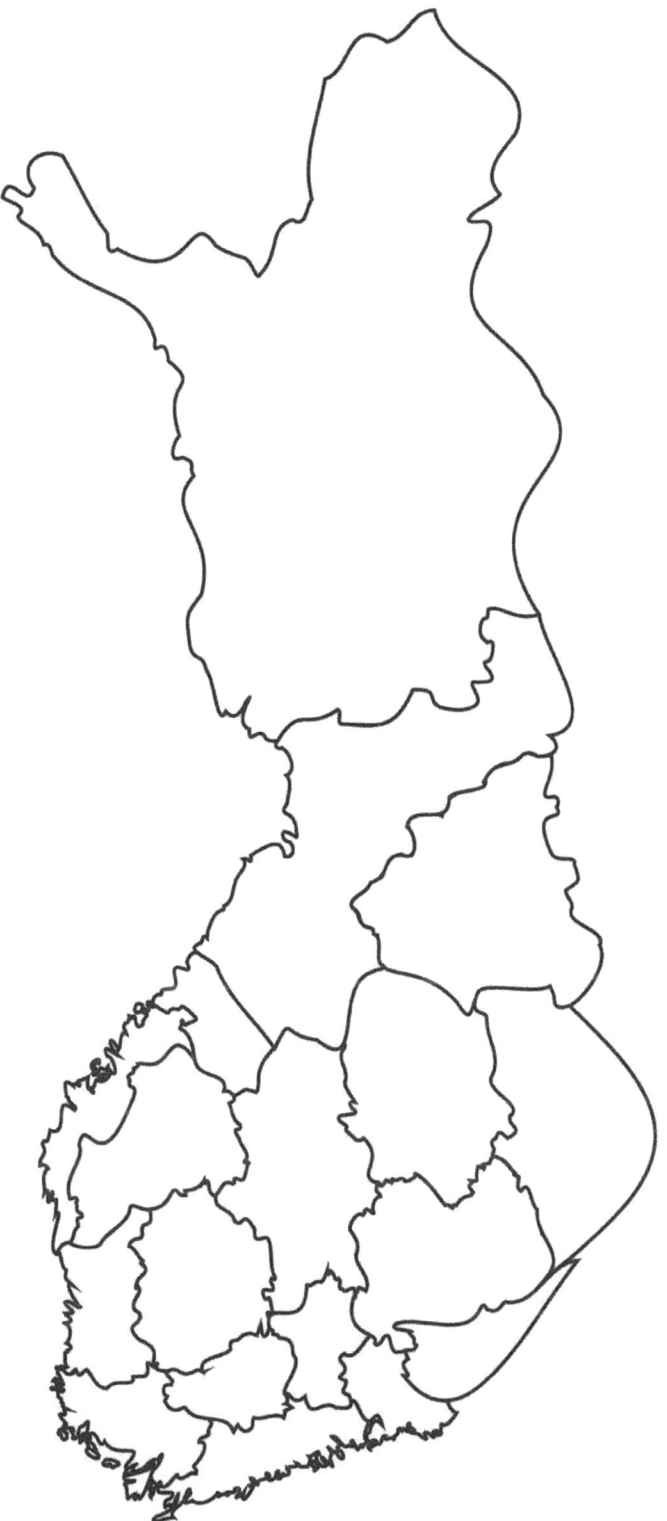

Outline Map of Europe

www.windyseapublishing.com   *Windy Sea Publishing*

Emotion Identification Cards

Cut out the cards and shuffle them. Then have students identify the emotion each character is displaying. Ask: What clues are there (in the character's face or body language) to tell you how he is feeling?

All images by Ugur Kose © Windy Sea Publishing, LLC

www.windyseapublishing.com

Windy Sea Publishing

Behavioral Cards

Cut out the cards, front and back together, as one unit. Fold the card in the middle and tape it closed. Use these cards with the Day 3 Lesson.

Bragging

Talking about yourself in a way that shows off.

Teasing

Making fun of someone in a mean way.

Teasing

Making fun of someone in a mean way.

Pranking

Tricks or jokes played on someone thought to be funny.

Pranking (Tricking)

Tricks or jokes played on someone thought to be funny.

Bragging

Talking about yourself in a way that shows off.

All images by Ugur Kose © Windy Sea Publishing, LLC

Helping (Caring)

Helping

Playing

All images by Ugur Kose © Windy Sea Publishing, LLC

Matching Worksheet Answer Keys

Opposites Matching

1. Bragging – D

2. Confused – F

3. Delicious – B

4. Clever – G

5. Miserable – A

6. Teased – C

7. Emerged – E

Vocabulary Matching

1. Pranks — A

2. Bragging — F

3. Nibbled — I

4. Confused — B

5. Delicious — E

6. Plotted — G

7. Clever — D

8. Miserable — H

9. Teased — C

10. Emerged — J

About the Authors

Betty Cetas taught first and second grades for several years until moving to Australia with her husband. After returning to the United States, she continued teaching in Sunday school classes, Bible studies, and imparting life lessons through her stories. She enjoys traveling and especially loved the log cottage she bought in the remote woods of Finland, where she spent summers with her family and friends, telling fanciful stories of provincial trolls, shy moose, and impish fish. She lives in Tucson, AZ with her husband and little dog, Abby, and summers in the woods in Williams, AZ.

Amanda M. Cetas is the author of the award-winning historical fiction adventure series, *A Country for Castoffs.* She was inspired to write these stories from two decades of researching her own family history. She taught diverse grade-level and Advanced Placement courses in American, European and World history to high school and middle school students for fourteen years. Amanda lives with her husband and two little Yorkie mixes. She has three grown children and four amazing grandchildren to keep her active!

Other books with accompanying teacher resources

Ages 4-8:

Oscar and the Awful, Horrible Smell
Oscar and the Noisy Children
Moe and the Tree Climbers (Coming Summer 2025)
Otto and the Lost Children (Coming Spring 2026)

Middle Grade/Young Adult:

Thrown to the Wind (Ages 9-12)
A Home in the Wilderness (11-13)
At the Mercy of the Sea (YA)
Charting a New Course (Coming in 2026)

www.ingramcontent.com/pod-product-compliance
Lightning Source LLC
Chambersburg PA
CBHW041131120626
46547CB00019B/2950